HO
ALL TIME FAVOURITE JOKE BOOK

Francesca Simon spent her childhood on the beach in California, and then went to Yale and Oxford Universities to study medieval history and literature. She now lives in London with her family. She has written over 50 books and won the Children's Book of the Year in 2008 at the Galaxy British Book Awards for *Horrid Henry and the Abominable Snowman*.

Tony Ross is one of Britain's best known illustrators, with many picture books to his name as well as line drawings for many fiction titles.

Also by Francesca Simon

Don't Cook Cinderella
Helping Hercules

and for younger readers

Café at the Edge of the Moon
Don't Be Horrid, Henry
Mr P's Naughty Book
The Parent Swap Shop
Spider School
The Topsy-Turvies

For a full list of **HORRID HENRY** titles,
visit www.horridhenry.co.uk.

You can also visit **HORRID HENRY's**
website for competitions, games,
downloads and a monthly newsletter!

HORRID HENRY'S
ALL TIME
FAVOURITE
JOKE BOOK

Francesca Simon
Illustrated by Tony Ross

Orion
Children's Books

First published in Great Britain in 2012
by Orion Children's Books
a division of the Orion Publishing Group Ltd
Orion House
5 Upper Saint Martin's Lane
London WC2H 9EA
An Hachette UK Company

7 9 10 8 6

Text © Francesca Simon 2012
Illustrations © Tony Ross 2012

Jokes compiled by Sally Byford.

The Orion Publishing Group's policy is to use papers
that are natural, renewable and recyclable products and
made from wood grown in sustainable forests. The logging
and manufacturing processes are expected to conform
to the environmental regulations of the country of origin.

ISBN 978 1 4440 0445 8

A catalogue record for this book is available from the British Library.

CONTENTS

HELLO FROM HENRY

Tee hee! Just when your parents and annoying brothers and sisters thought they'd heard all of your mega-watt killer jokes, my all time best joke book is here to save the day. These fantastically funny jokes will guarantee non-stop laughs. Why should you have to listen to boring story CDs in the car when everyone can listen to YOU instead? Purple Hand Gang - Henry's ultimate, deluxe, super-whopper mega joke book has arrived.

Keep laughing!

Henry

HORRID HENRY'S TOP TEN BONKERS BEASTS

What do you get if you sit under a cow?
A pat on the head.

Why don't leopards cheat in exams?
Because they know they'll be spotted.

How does an elephant get down from a tree?
He sits on a leaf and waits for it to fall.

*What's worse than an elephant with
a sore trunk?*
A centipede with sore feet.

*When is it bad luck to be followed
by a black cat?*
When you're a mouse.

Why do giraffes have long necks?
Because their feet smell.

What's orange and sounds like a parrot?
A carrot.

When's the best time to buy a bird?
When it's going "cheep cheep".

*What do you get when you cross
a sheep with a kangaroo?*
A woolly jumper.

Waiter, waiter, do you serve fish?
Sit down, sir, we serve anyone.

DAFT DOCTORS

Doctor, Doctor, I swallowed a dictionary.
Don't breathe a word to anyone.

Doctor, Doctor, I can't feel my legs!
That's because I've cut off your arms.

Doctor, Doctor, I think I'm a little overweight.
Nonsense, pull up three chairs and we'll
talk about it.

Doctor, Doctor, how can I stop feeling run-down?
Try looking both ways before you cross the road.

What do you call someone who sits in a doctor's waiting room for hours and hours?
Patient.

Where do ships go when they are ill?
To the docks.

Doctor, Doctor, I swallowed a bone.
Are you choking?
No, I really did.

Doctor, Doctor, how do I stop my nose from running?
Stick your foot out and trip it up.

Doctor, Doctor, I feel like a pack of cards.
I'll deal with you later.

Doctor, Doctor, my sister thinks she's a lift.
Well, tell her to come and see me.
She can't – she doesn't stop at this floor.

Doctor, Doctor, I snore so loudly
I keep myself awake.
Sleep in another room then.

Doctor, Doctor, when I press with my
finger here, it hurts – and when I press
here, it hurts – and here and here.
What's wrong with me?
You've got a broken finger!

COMPUTER CRACK-UPS

Why did the computer go to the doctor's?
It had a nasty virus.

*Why did the
computer
wear glasses?*
To improve
its website.

What do computers have to look after?
Their pet mouse.

Why did the boy eat his computer?
Because it was an Apple.

What did the computer do at the beach?
It put on screensaver and surfed the net.

You Tube, Twitter, and Facebook are making a joint website. What's it going to be called?
You-Twit-Face.

Why did the computer go to a shoe shop?
Because it was rebooting.

Why was the computer overweight?
It was always taking megabytes.

What do you call a computer superhero?
A screen saver.

How did the computer criminal get out of jail?
He pressed the escape key.

What do computers eat?
Microchips.

What do you get when you cross
a computer with an elephant?
Lots of memory.

BONKERS
BIRTHDAYS

*What do you say to the toothless granny
on her birthday?*
Many gappy returns.

DAD: Would you like a pocket
calculator for your birthday?
HORRID HENRY: No, thanks.
I already know how many pockets
I've got.

What do you sing to an alien who's just arrived on this planet?
Happy Earth-day to You.

HORRID HENRY: I've got my eye on that big shiny bike for my birthday.
DAD: Well, you'd better keep your eye on it, because you'll never get your bottom on it.

MUM: Did you like the dictionary I gave you for your birthday?
PERFECT PETER: Yes, I've been trying to find the words to thank you.

DAD: I'm trying to buy a present for my son. Can you help me out?
SHOP ASSISTANT: Certainly, sir. Which way did you come in?

What did the bald man say when he got a comb for his birthday?
Thanks, I'll never part with it.

Knock knock.
Who's there?
Rabbit.
Rabbit who?
Rabbit up neatly. It's a birthday present.

What's the best birthday present in the world?
A broken drum, you can't beat it!

What's the best birthday present for a skeleton?
A mobile bone.

What do you give a gorilla for his birthday?
I don't know, but let's hope he likes it!

BLECCCCH! VALENTINE'S DAY

What did the finger say to the thumb?
People will say we're in glove.

What did the bee say to the flower?
Hi, honey!

What did the girl octopus say to the boy octopus?
I want to hold your hand, hand, hand,
hand, hand, hand, hand, hand.

*What do farmers give their wives on
Valentine's Day?*
Hogs and kisses.

Why did the boy bat fall in love with the girl bat?
Because she was fun to hang around with.

Did you hear about the short-sighted hedgehog?
She fell in love with a hairbrush.

Why is lettuce the most romantic vegetable?
Because it's all heart.

What kind of flowers did Henry give
Margaret on Valentine's Day?
Cauliflowers.

Who is Dracula most likely to
fall in love with?
The girl necks
door.

Knock knock.
Who's there?
Olive.
Olive who?
Olive you.

Why did the acrobats get married?
They were head over heels in love.

Knock knock.
Who's there?
Howard.
Howard who?
Howard you like a big kiss.

What do you call a very small Valentine?
A Valentiny.

What did the girl volcano say to the boy volcano on Valentine's Day?
I lava you.

EASTER EGGSTRAVAGANZA

*What happens when you throw eggs
at a Dalek?*
It's eggs-terminated!

*Why did Greedy Graham laugh at his
fried egg?*
He thought it was a really funny yolk.

Why did the chicken carry an umbrella?
The weather was foul.

*What happened when the chicken ate a
big pile of sage, onion and breadcrumbs?*
It was stuffed.

*What happens when you take the yolk
out of an egg?*
It's all white.

t did Mr and Mrs Chicken
their baby?
~~g.~~

Why does E. T. like omelettes?
Because he's an Eggs-tra Terrestrial.

What does Father Christmas do at Easter?
Nothing. He egg-nores the whole
thing.

Why shouldn't you tell a joke to an
Easter egg?
It might crack up.

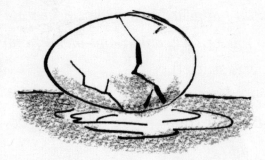

What's a chicken's favourite TV programme?
The feather forecast.

Doctor, Doctor, I think I'm a chicken.
How long has this been going on?
Ever since I was an egg.

*What do you get when you cross
a chicken with a thief?*
A peck-pocket.

Why couldn't the chicken find her eggs?
She mislaid them.

How do you catch a rabbit?
Hide behind a tree and make a noise
like a carrot.

SPORTING SILLIES

Why did the winning football team spin their trophy round and round?
It was the Whirled Cup.

When was the first tennis match in space played?
A lawn time ago in a galaxy far away.

What do you get if you cross martial arts with soccer?
Kung fu-tball.

*ose job is it to carry the cricket players
each match?*
The coach.

Why did the footballer play in his kitchen?
It was a home game.

What lights up a football stadium?
A football match.

*Why did the footballer run out of salt
and pepper?*
It was the end of the seasoning.

Why did the snooker player feel off colour?
He wasn't getting enough greens.

What's the angriest part of the goal?
The crossbar.

What does Kung-Fu Kate like to eat?
Karate chops.

What did the footballer say when he burped during a game?
Sorry, it was a freak hic.

Why was the football stadium so chilly?
It was full of fans.

Which type of gymnastics are sheep best at?
The asymmetric baaaaas.

LAZY LINDA: I've just seen the doctor and he says I can't play netball.
MISS BATTLE-AXE: Oh, he's seen you play too, has he?

Did you hear about the goalie with the piggy bank?
He was always saving.

Why didn't the dog play badminton?
Because he was a boxer.

Why did the football pitch become a triangle?
Somebody took a corner.

Why should you leave Aerobic Al's trainers well alone?
They're not to be sniffed at.

If you have a referee in football, a referee in rugby and a referee in boxing, what do you have in bowls?
Pudding.

Why was the octopus a good footballer?
Because of his ten-tackles.

HOLIDAY HOWLERS

What do you say to someone who's climbed to the top of a mountain?
Hi!

What do double agents play when they go on holiday?
I spy.

*Where did Moody Margaret go on holiday
this year?*
Alaska.
Don't worry, I'll ask her myself.

Where do zombies go on holiday?
The Deaditerranean.

*If I'm standing at the North Pole, facing the
South Pole, and the east is on my left, what's
on my right hand?*
Your fingers.

Doctor, Doctor, I keep thinking I'm an alien. Nonsense, you just need a holiday. You're right – I've heard Mars is nice this time of year.

MISS BATTLE-AXE: What did you learn during the summer holidays, Henry?
HORRID HENRY: That seven weeks isn't long enough to tidy my bedroom.

DAD: I hate to say this, but your swimming costume is very tight.
MUM: Wear your own then.

Why did the clown throw cream pies at the audience?
It was jest for fun.

DAD: Did you enjoy your trip to the seaside?
HORRID HENRY: No – a crab bit my toe!
DAD: Which one?
HORRID HENRY: I don't know – all crabs look the same to me.

MAN: I'd like a return ticket, please.
CLERK: Certainly, sir. Where to?
MAN: Back here, of course.

How is the sea held in place?
It's tied.

Why did the monkey sunbathe?
To get an orangu-tan.

FUNNY
FOOD

How do you know a sausage doesn't like being fried?
Because it spits!

What do you get when you cross roast pork with a telephone?
Crackling on the line.

What stays hot, even in the fridge?
Mustard.

What does Horrid Henry call Perfect Peter when he's stepped in syrup?
Gooey-Two-Shoes.

Why is a tomato round and red?
Because if it was long and green it would be a cucumber.

What do you get when you cross a pig with a centipede?
Bacon and legs.

CUSTOMER: Get me something to eat and make it snappy!
WAITER: How about a crocodile sandwich?

If you have five potatoes, how do you share them between three people?
Mash them.

Where do you learn how
to make ice cream?
Sundae school.

Why did the banana peel?
It forgot to put on any sun cream.

Why did Greedy Graham eat his dinner
with a spade?
He likes to shovel it down.

Why do aliens have trouble drinking tea?
Because of the flying saucers.

Why was the banana afraid to snore?
In case it woke up the rest of the bunch.

AEROBIC AL: I'm going swimming after my lunch.
HORRID HENRY: Really, I'm getting mine from the take-away.

CLASSROOM CHAOS

A man escaped from prison by digging a tunnel under his cell. When he emerged, he was in the middle of a school playground. "I'm free!" cried the man. "So what?" said a little girl. "I'm four."

HORRID HENRY: Miss, my pen's run out.
MISS BATTLE-AXE: Well, go and chase after it then.

Why are school chips like a history lesson? Because you get to discover ancient grease.

MISS BATTLE-AXE: Give me a sentence using the word "fascinate".
SOUR SUSAN: My coat has ten buttons, but I can only fasten eight.

MISS BATTLE-AXE: Why have you painted black and white squares all over the computer screen?
HORRID HENRY: I wanted to check my emails.

What's easy to get into at school, but hard to get out of?
Trouble.

Why was Horrid Henry's packed lunch so stinky?
It had passed its smell-by-date.

MISS BATTLE-AXE: Where is Timbuktu?
HORRID HENRY: Between Timbuk-one and Timbuk-three.

MISS BATTLE-AXE: You're late again, Henry. What's your excuse this time?
HORRID HENRY: I ran here so fast, I didn't have time to think of one.

BRAINY BRIAN: Dad, Dad, I got an A in spelling.

DAD: Don't be silly, Brian! There's isn't an A in spelling.

Why did Beefy Bert spread glue on his head? To help things stick in his mind.

MISS BATTLE-AXE: Give me a sentence using the word "benign".

HORRID HENRY: This year, I'll be eight – but next year I benign.

MISS BATTLE-AXE: Why are you crawling into school? And you're ten minutes late!

HORRID HENRY: Well, you said you didn't want to see me walking in late again.

MISS BATTLE-AXE: Can you name two birds that can't fly?

HORRID HENRY: An ostrich and a dead parrot.

HORRID HENRY: I'm phoning to say I won't be able to come to school today.
MISS BATTLE-AXE: Why not?
HORRID HENRY: I've lost my voice.

Which word of five letters has six left when you take two away?
Sixty.

MISS BATTLE-AXE: If I cut three apples, four oranges and two pears into ten pieces each, what will I have?
GREEDY GRAHAM: A fruit salad.

TOUGH TOBY: I want to be a rubbish collector when I grow up.
MISS BATTLE-AXE: But you haven't got any experience.
TOUGH TOBY: I'll just pick it up as I go along.

MEGA MONEY

Why did Henry put his money in the freezer?
He wanted cold, hard cash.

How much did the pirate's earrings cost?
A buccaneer.

What's the quickest way to double your money?
Fold it in half.

What do you get if you cross a sorceress with a millionaire?
A very witch person.

Why is money called dough?
Because we all knead it.

HORRID HENRY: What would you do if a bull charged you?
ANXIOUS ANDREW: I'd pay whatever it charged.

What happened when Fluffy swallowed a pound?
There was money in the kitty.

MR MOSSY: You're very quiet today, Henry.

HORRID HENRY: Well, Mum gave me a pound not to say anything about your red nose.

Why did Robin Hood steal money from the rich? Because the poor didn't have any.

DAFT DINOSAURS

What do you do with a green dinosaur?
Wait till it ripens.

What do dinosaurs put on their chips?
Tomatosaurus.

What does a Triceratops sit on?
Its Tricera–bottom.

*What do you get when you cross a dinosaur
with a lemon?*
A dino-sour.

*What do you call a dinosaur that left its
armour out in the rain?*
A stegosaurust.

*What do you call a dinosaur that never gives
up?*
A try-try-try-ceratops.

*What do you call a dinosaur
wearing high heels?*
My-feet-are-saurus.

What do you call a dinosaur who is always walking in the mud?
Brown–toe–saurus.

When can three giant dinosaurs hide under an umbrella and not get wet?
When it's not raining.

Why do people avoid dinosaurs?
Because their eggs stink.

MONSTER
MANIA

What does the polite monster say when he meets people for the first time?
Pleased to eat you.

Why was the monster called Fog?
Because he was thick and grey.

How do you greet a three-headed monster?
Hello, hello, hello.

Why did the monster cross the road?
To eat the chicken.

The police are looking for a monster with one eye.
Why don't they use two?

What did the monster eat at Restaurant Le Posh?
The waiter.

What do you call an alien with three eyes?
Aliiien.

How do monsters cook their food?
They terror-fry it.

What is an ogre's favourite flavour squash?
Lemon and slime.

What do monsters like best for pudding?
Eyes-cream.

What do you call a monster with no neck?
The Lost Neck Monster.

*What time was it when the monster
swallowed the Prime Minister?*
Ate P.M.

*What do you call a monster with a big hairy
nose, pointed yellow teeth and red eyes?*
Ugly.

*What do you call a monster with a big
hairy nose, pointed yellow teeth, red eyes
and no legs?*
Still ugly.

ANIMAL MADNESS

What goes "stomp, stomp, stomp, squelch"?
An elephant wearing wet trainers.

What do you get if you cross a chicken with a guitar?
A hen that makes music when you pluck it.

Two elephants walked off a cliff ...

Boom! Boom!

Why don't you see penguins in Great Britain?
Because they're afraid of Wales.

Have you got any dogs going cheap?
No, all mine go "Woof".

A man took his dog to the vet, and said, "My dog is cross-eyed – is there anything you can do?"

The vet picked up the dog and carefully examined him. Finally, he said, "I'm going to have to put him down."

"Why?" said the man. "Just because he's cross-eyed?"

"No," said the vet. "Because he's very heavy."

What do you get when you cross a monkey with a flower?
A chimp-pansy.

*What do you call one bee with another bee
on its back?*
A double-decker buzz.

*What do you get when you cross a cow
with a duck?*
Cream quackers.

*What do you get when you cross a parrot
with a shark?*
An animal that talks your head off.

Where would you find a dog with no legs?
Exactly where you left it.

Which is richer? A cow or a bull?
A bull – because the cow gives you
milk, but the bull charges.

*What kind of cheese would you use to disguise
a horse?*
Mascarpone.

What kind of dog is always in a hurry?
A dash-hound.

Why was the bee's hair sticky?
Because he used a honey-comb.

What did the goose get when he was cold?
People-pimples.

What do you get when you cross a mouse with an orange?
A pipsqueak.

What's the difference between a well-dressed man and a tired dog?
The man wears a suit – the dog just pants.

HALLOWE'EN HOOTS

What happens when a ghost gets a fright?
He jumps into his skin.

What's the scariest squidgiest day of the year?
Marshmallowe'en.

What's a vampire's favourite kind of ice cream?
Vein-illa.

What did one ghost say to the other ghost?
"Do you believe in people?"

What do you call a vampire who likes to relax in a bloodbath with a good book?
Well red.

What do you do when fifty zombies surround your house?
Hope it's Hallowe'en.

Why didn't the witch wear a flat cap?
There was no point.

What is as sharp as a vampire's fang?
His other fang.

How do you join the Dracula fan club?
Send your name, address and blood group.

What kind of jewellery do witches wear?
Charm bracelets.

Do zombies eat crisps with their fingers?
No, they eat the fingers separately.

*What happens when a ghost
gets lost in the fog?*
He is mist.

What kind of make-up do witches wear?
Mas–scare–a.

*What's the difference between a deer
running away and a small witch?*
One's a hunted stag, the other's
a stunted hag.

CRAZY CREEPY-CRAWLIES

SLUG: Who's that sitting on your back?
SNAIL: That's Michelle.

How deep is the water in a pond full of frogs?
Knee-deep, knee-deep, knee-deep.

How do you know which end of a worm is its head?
Tickle it and see which end smiles.

What does a toad say when he sees something he likes?
"That's toad–ally awesome!"

Why don't baby birds ever smile?
Because their mothers feed them worms all day.

Where do you find giant snails?
On the end of a giant's fingers.

How do frogs do DIY?
With toad's tools.

What is a tadpole after it is five days old?
Six days old.

What lies on the ground, a hundred feet in the air?
A centipede.

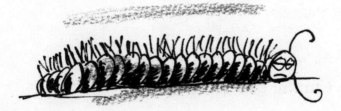

REALLY
RUDE

Why couldn't the knickers do any magical tricks?
They were just pants.

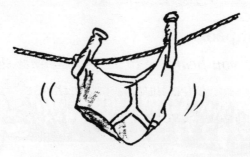

Knock knock.
Who's there?
Henrietta.
Henrietta who?
Henrietta bogey!

What's got a bottom at the top?
A toilet.

Did you hear about the grandfather clock
that was filled with mouldy cheese?
It ponged every hour.

What do you get if you cross ten aliens with Humpty Dumpty?
Ten green bottoms hanging on a wall.

What happened to the thief who stole a lorry load of knicker elastic?
He was sent to prison for a long stretch.

Which queen burped a lot?
Queen Hic-toria.

Which king had a noisy bottom?
Richard the Lionfart.

Knock knock.
Who's there?
Nicholas.
Nicholas who?
Nicholas girls shouldn't climb trees.

*What's brown and sounds
like a bell?*
Dung.

What's the rudest vegetable?
A pea.

*What's hairy,
scary and
wears knickers
on its head?*
The Under-werewolf.

Who shouted knickers at the big bad wolf?
Little Rude Riding Hood.

Why do gorillas have big nostrils?
Because they have big fingers.

MOODY MOANERS

What do you call a sad spaceship?
An unidentified crying object.

Have you ever seen a fish cry?
No, but I've seen a whale blubber.

What happened when Fluffy the cat ate a lemon?
She became a sourpuss.

What's Moody Margaret's favourite day of the week?
Moanday.

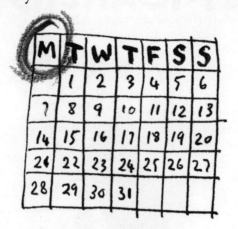

Why was the maths book in a bad mood?
It had a lot of problems.

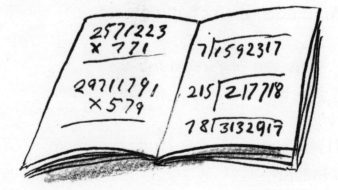

Why are adults always complaining?
Because they are groan-ups.

Which painting is always grumpy?
The Moaning Lisa.

Why did the cow have sour milk?
Because she was mooooody.

CHRISTMAS CRACKERS

What do you call a reindeer who won't say please and thank you?
Rude-olph.

Where did the mistletoe go to become rich and famous?
Hollywood.

What bird has wings but can't fly?
A roast turkey.

What do snowmen sing at parties?
Freeze a jolly good fellow?

*What jumps from cake to cake and tastes
of almonds?*
Tarzipan.

Where do ghosts go for a Christmas treat?
The phantomime.

Have you heard the story of the three reindeer?
No, I haven't.
Oh dear, dear, dear.

What kind of bread do elves use to make sandwiches?
Shortbread.

ELF: Santa, the reindeer swallowed my pencil. What should I do?
SANTA: Use a pen.

Where is the best place to put your Christmas tree?
Between your Christmas two and your Christmas four.

*What did the sheep say
to the shepherd?*
Season's
bleatings.

How long should an elf's legs be?
Just long enough to reach the ground.

*How does Rudolph know
when Christmas
is coming?*
He looks
at his
calen–deer.

What's the best thing to give your parents at Christmas?
A list of everything you want.